FRANK MEADOW SUTCLIFFE

Hon F.R.P.S

Whitby and its people as seen by one of the founders of the naturalistic movement in photography.

A selection of his work compiled by Bill Eglon Shaw.

The Sutcliffe Gallery,
Whitby, North Yorkshire,
England.

First published 1974
First re-print 1975
Second re-print 1976
Third re-print 1982 (amended and improved)
Fourth re-print 1985

Published and © 1985 by:

The Sutcliffe Gallery
1 Flowergate, Whitby, North Yorkshire, YO21 3BA,
England   Tel: Whitby (0947) 602239
by agreement with Whitby Literary & Philosophical Society

The book printed by
Jayscale Duotone Offset at
the printing house of
John S. Speight Limited
a division of Hawthornes of Nottingham Limited
Parkside Works, Guiseley, Leeds LS20 8BH

ISBN   0 9503175 0 0

INTRODUCTION

This is a picture book. Some of the pictures have interesting facts attached to them. But primarily it is intended to show two things. Firstly, that a man carrying a cumbersome camera and heavy plate holders could produce photographs, not cumbersome, but which were elegantly composed and sensitively conceived; not heavy but containing in them the essence of light and lightness.

Secondly, it condenses an era and a place into images easily comprehended, and, if viewed often enough and long enough these images will begin to draw one back in time to become part of them; to feel with, and for, the people of that time; to grasp the harshness yet tranquility of those lives.

We owe a deep and lasting gratitude to Frank Meadow Sutcliffe that he has enabled us to do these things. An artist who chose to use a camera as his medium, his work has an immediacy and truth not so readily captured with brush or pencil.

Sutcliffe did not duffuse his talents. Although Whitby was geographically isolated, with access to the rest of the country not an easy matter, this was not the only reason why the port and its immediate surroundings formed the subject matter for the vast majority of his photographs. His obvious love for the place and its people found expression in his work and this may be seen time and again in the examples chosen for this book.

In addition to Whitby itself the neighbouring fishing villages of Staithes, Runswick, Sandsend and Robin Hood's Bay and the surrounding farming areas of the Esk Valley and North Yorkshire Moors are all sympathetically portrayed.

The book was first published in 1974 in response to the very many requests we had received over a number of years for a collection of Sutcliffe's photographs in book form. The problem was whether to make a cheaply printed catalogue with indifferently reproduced illustrations or to produce an edition to the highest standards. The latter format was chosen as it was felt that the delicate gradation and subtle tones could so easily be lost by inferior reproduction techniques.

Photogravure was the process decided upon in 1974 but due to advances made during the intervening years in duotone photolithography, both in the USA by the Rapoport Corporation and in this country by John S. Speight Ltd., the decision was made to change to this process.

The present book is rather more than a re-print as new process negatives and plates have had to be produced to accommodate the different requirements of photolithography.

At the same time an improvement has been made in the layout of the book and a number of minor errors in captioning have been corrected.

The photographs were taken between 1870 and around 1910 during which period photographic materials progressed from the wet collodian process with glass plates coated by the photographer immediately prior to the photograph being taken, to the more standardised factory-made dry plate, introduced around 1880. Partly because of this the negatives vary considerably in quality.

The duotone plates used when printing this book were made from modern photographic prints taken, with very few exceptions, from the original whole plate (6½'' × 8½'') negatives. Two of the exceptions, illustrations 31-25B and 31-26A (pages nine and twelve respectively), are from half plate glass negatives which are thought to be copies of original Kodak roll film negatives taken towards the end of the century.

Very little documentation of the negatives has survived from Sutcliffe's time and it is only research over the past years that has enabled us to give captions to many of the photographs. This information is given in good faith but no responsibility is accepted for any errors or omissions.

Titles printed in double quotation marks are those given by Frank Sutcliffe. Words in single quotes are either boat names or the nicknames of people.

The poem ''Homage to F. M. Sutcliffe'' by Tom Stamp on page 63 is reproduced by courtesy of the author to whom sincere thanks are given.

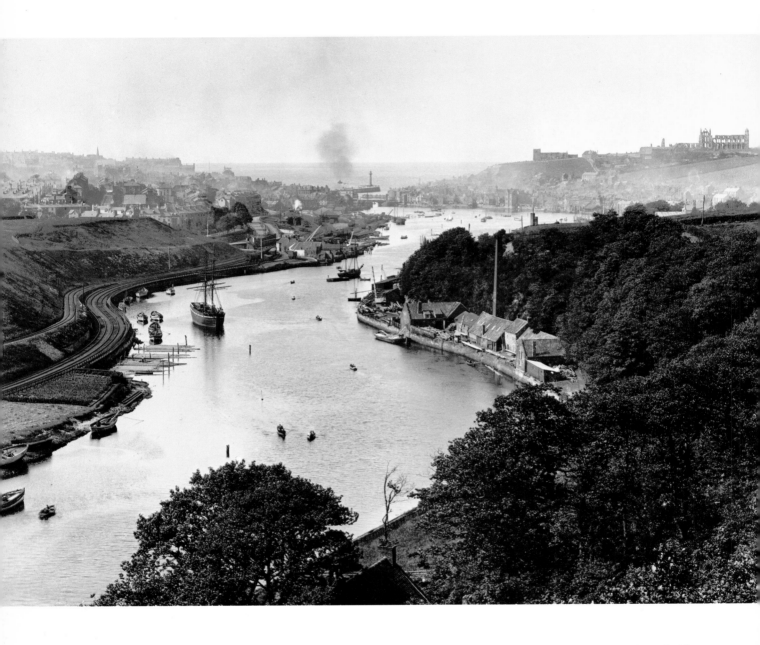

Many of Sutcliffe's photographs were taken within the areas visible on the picture above and the lower one opposite. Above, looking northwards towards the sea are the lower reaches of the River Esk and Whitby town whose east and west sides are joined by the swing bridge which divides the upper and lower harbour. The Abbey ruins and St. Mary's Parish Church are on the horizon towards the right. The group of buildings (since demolished) on the right bank of the river in the mid-distance was a Prussian Blue dye works.   13-49B

The top illustration opposite shows a cottage, the roof of which can be seen in the foreground above. The well sheltered moorings for smaller boats on this stretch of the Esk were particularly valuable during very rough weather and when work was being carried out on the craft.   18-1A.

In the lower photograph, looking inland from a similar viewpoint to that used above are Whitby Gas Works, built in the mid 1800s on the site where blubber-boiling houses stood during the whale fishing days; the Whitby-Pickering railway line alongside the river and above it, along the hillside, the line joining Whitby Town and West Cliff Stations. The factory building in the distance beyond the Gas Works was Batt's Foundry established in 1853 by Mr Robert Hutton where such items as ovens, boilers, ranges, turnip cutters and North Cave Plough metals were manufactured. This view is now dominated by the railway viaduct built in the early 1880s.   25-41C.

"Confidences." Whitby fishergirls at the foot of the cliffs. 18-45D.

A Whitby fisherman. 26-2B.

Nell 'Baccus' or Bakehouse. 3-69B.

'Stumper' Dryden and Tom Langlands. 17-47B.

A Norwegian Jakt, the 'Hanna' of Mandal (a small port on the southern-most tip of Norway) about to pass through the swing bridge into the upper harbour.   19-36B.

Town and lower harbour from Spion Kop. The bridge was completed in 1835 at a cost of £10,000 and replaced in 1908 by the present bridge on the same site.   17-22B.

A lugger from Blyth, Northumberland, moored at the quayside.   16-13B.

Nets hanging to dry on Scottish luggers from Montrose and Peterhead. D10B.

The brigantine 'Astrea' of 286 tons, a coastal trader which plied weekly between Chamberlain's Wharf, London and ports on the north-east coast, against the quayside. In the background are brigs moored over-winter in the upper harbour. The two most prominent ones are Southampton boats. 10-53B.

Becalmed off the coast. A brigantine being towed into Whitby harbour. 31-25B.

Two fishermen, one of them 'Stumper' Dryden, against cobles beached on Langborne Sands, upper harbour. 10-41B.

The 'Diamond' of Scarborough, owned by Captain William McLean, unloading coal from either Blyth or Hartlepool into carts on Sandsend beach. Advertisement in Whitby Times of 25th November 1887: Good and Cheap! Best Household Coals are now selling on board the brig 'Ebenezer' lying at the New Quay, at 14/- per ton cash, or 11d per bag. Orders received at the Ship or James Ward, Schooner Inn, Whitby.' C-18D.

St. Ann's Staith, with Pier Road in the distance. 28-18B.

Cobles and Scottish luggers in the upper harbour. 26-26A.

Skaning mussels, Tate Hill. Girl in spotted blouse, Amelia Peart; girl looking towards left, Lizzie Alice Hawksfield. 19-21C.

"The Mudlarks." Tate Hill Sands. 18-36B.

"From the Deep Blue Sea to a Clothes Basket." The Fish Market, Coffee House End, Whitby. 24-23B.

One of the few artificially staged photographs, presumably depicting a smugglers' den. Left to right: Tim Ward of Staithes; William Moat, fisherman of The Cragg, Whitby; 'Luscall' Jack, street sweeper and odd-job man. 4-39B.

The Storm family of Robin Hood's Bay with their coble 'Gratitude'. Left to right: Thomas, Reuben, Matthew, Spy the dog and Isaac, the father who was cox of the lifeboat. Circa 1895.   31-26A.

Boats moored against quayside, Whitby upper harbour.   20-25B.

"The Critic." Group with lobster pots on Tate Hill Pier. The boy is George Walker, man on left John 'Batch' Batchelor and on right 'Cud' Colley. Circa 1908. B-38A.

Group on Tate Hill beach.   16-27B.

"Repairs." Runswick Bay.   24-28B.

"Dock End." On the right is the 'Alert', built at Whitby in 1802 by G. & L. Langborne as a sloop and later converted to a schooner. In 1880 when the photograph was taken she was owned by Anthony Jackson and Edward Barker. Lying at the left are the 'Lively', 'Sara' and 'Hopewell'.   B-17A.

The topsail schooner 'Anna' of 211 tons, built at Sunderland in 1845. Moored at Dock End. 19-48B.

'Northern Light', a hulk moored at Bog Hall. 4-25B.

S.S. 'Southwark' of London, blown ashore in a November gale in 1893 at Upgang, one mile from Whitby. A London firm contracted to refloat her. Sand was dug out to form a sea break. Heavy timbers were laid beneath her and hydraulic jacks used to slide her sufficiently far down the beach to enable her to be refloated. 17-37A.

Tug steamers 'Cleveland' and 'Nunthorpe' manoeuvre iron steamships towards the upper harbour through the swing bridge. At that time the bridge had a waterway of slightly over 45 feet leaving little room to spare for such vessels. B-13A (above)

2-70C (right)

"After Forty Years." Two old fisherfolk, thought to have been taken at Staithes. 10-8B.

At Cowbar end of Staithes footbridge. Margaret Verrill is bringing home two freshly baked loaves from the communal bakehouse which Staithes had at that time. She was to have married a fisherman named Billy Unthank, but he, together with his father and brother, were drowned on the day they were to have been married. She later married Thomas Ward Verrill. The men in the photograph are, l. to r., George Webster, 'Swaddy' Harrison and Ned Verrill. 3-93A.

Women going to gather flithers, or limpets, as bait for the fishing lines of their menfolk. On this photograph fuel, in the form of driftwood is also being collected. The fishermens' wives and daughters led lives as physically arduous as their menfolk, if not as dangerous, and they lived close to the poverty line much of the time, yet were by many accounts happier and more contented than many of today's considerably more affluent and 'liberated' women. Much of this had to do with the strong spirit of community and sense of purpose which existed amongst them. 18-31B.

Two flither pickers with buckets full of limpets on the Scaur, a rock beach off Whitby's East Cliff.   26-13A.

At the sea end of Henrietta Street, Whitby. 14-21B.

More flither pickers at work.   3-95A.

"What did you say, my dear, I'm a little hard of hearing." 26-10A.

Busy fingers at Whitby. 16-30A (detail).

Whitby fisherwomen making net. The skills required of women were many. 19-7B.

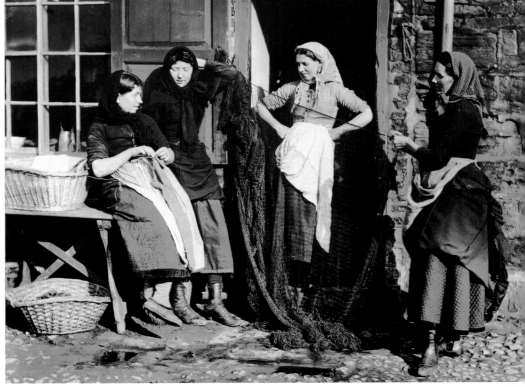

New Quay fish stall, Whitby. The man in the peaked cap was Tom Gaines who fished with the harbourmaster, John Knight, in the herring mule 'The Coffee Bar'. The woman on his right is his wife Dolly, a fish stall owner. On his left is Eliza Cummins. The stall was owned by Mrs Wilson, known locally as 'Nell Baccus', who is second from the left. At extreme left is Mrs Eleanor Locker.   B-30A.

More industry. Lace making and knitting whilst resting on the pier wall.   B16A.

Coast Guards on Battery Parade. In 1850 Whitby's complement was seven men and a mounted guard.   14-4A.

The Fish Pier and east side of the lower harbour. St. Mary's Parish Church on the skyline.   C-17C.

A peaceful scene in the upper harbour.   7-2C.

Polly Swallow — a studio portrait.   24-29C.

Almost certainly taken at Hull. The boat at the left is probably of Dutch origin. Next is the schooner 'Eliza' of Dublin. On her right is the 'Constance' of Falmouth. The names of the vessel to her right and of the steam ship cannot be distinguished. 11-5B.

Whitby upper harbour looking towards Sandgate. The interest here lies partly in the foreground of the photograph where two beds of mussels can be seen. These were brought from the River Tees, at that time relatively unpolluted, by fishing smacks, in an attempt to naturalise them at Whitby but this was unsuccessful. The stone enclosures were subsequently used to keep alive for a few days until required, mussels which had been gathered locally. 19-50B.

Cobles on the mud where formerly Mr Henry Barrick had a ship-building yard and a dry dock for carrying out repairs. In 1865 the North Eastern Railway Company bought this area and afterwards filled and levelled it obliterating all signs of the ship-building activities. The two large boats close together in the background are probably a brigantine partly obscured by a barque. 10-50A.

A rather studied group on Tate Hill Sands in Whitby lower harbour. The boat being painted is a clinker-built Yorkshire Coble, a design much favoured by Whitby fishermen and which at that time could be either rowed or sailed but which at the present time is often fitted with an inboard diesel engine. The coble was designed to be launched from a beach into the surf. The general shape, if not detailed construction, of this boat, reaches back thousands of years to the early Scandinavian boat builders.   19-13A.

Whitby Fish Market at Coffee House End. Men who have been identified, working from the left are; with book and wearing white round-crowned hat, Edward Turner, a fish merchant; next to him in peaked cap, Joseph Blackburn of Kiln Yard; with bowler hat and hands on hips, Christopher 'Kit' Eglon, fish auctioneer of Elephant and Castle Yard, Haggersgate and great-grandfather of the writer; next to him, pipe in mouth, 'Bill Tom' Winspear; in uniform, Naval Reservist 'Jolka' Eglon of The Cragg; the two men at right are Robert Coulson and Robert Hansell, fishermen, both of whom were later drowned at sea.   B-28A.

"An Unwilling Pupil." Taken on Tate Hill Pier.   24-20B.

Whitby from St. Mary's Parish Church.   13-35A.

A restful scene in the lower harbour.   B-33C.

'Lively' and 'Mulgrave' at Bog Hall.   17-34B.

Tate Hill Beach with Henrietta Street in the background.   20-29B.

The 166 ton snow 'Opal' of Whitby. She was built at Greenock in 1845 and first registered at Whitby in 1865, the owners at that time being Jonathan Skerry and John Hesp. Later, in 1893 she was owned by George and Will Hopper. In December 1867 she went ashore at Dieppe under Captain James Power. In 1899 she was sold to the Cleveland Flour Mills Company for use as a lighter.   3-55A.

Girl knitting at the end of Whitby's West Pier.   B-2C.

Fisherman and boy on cliff-top. Both have the type of hooked lines used by long-line fishermen.   14-39A.

Fishermen on Tate Hill Pier.   D-14B.

Taken on the New Quay, Whitby. Harry Freeman at the left.   B-5C.

Fishing boats in the upper harbour.
20-18B.

Whitby fishermen. Th[...]
steps have since bee[...]
covered by an extensio[...]
to the pier.   E-19A.

View up the lower harbour from Scotch
Head. The block of buildings at the bridge
end in the centre of the photograph was
demolished during the late 1970s. On the
end of one of the buildings on Marine
Parade, towards the right of centre, is
painted 'The Whitby Jet Works — Wm.
Wright — Proprietor'. During the latter
half of the nineteenth century the jet
ornament industry employed over a
thousand men and boys in Whitby.
24-13B.

Henry Freeman, lifeboatman for over forty years and sole survivor of the Whitby Lifeboat Disaster of 1861 when twelve men were drowned close by the West Pier. He died in December 1904.   24-30D.

A net drying from the mast of a coble beached on the 'Little Sands' on the west side of the lower harbour. A sunny day, but the north-east wind would be keeping things cool! 4-15C.

Coastguards photographed in the studio. 6-92B.

High seas breaking over the end of the West Pier. An account of taking photographs under similar stormy conditions is described by Sutcliffe in Michael Hiley's biography on the photographer. Of interest is the low rail running along the right hand side of the pier which was used as a rubbing strip for the rope used by gangs of men to tow up the harbour sailing boats which were becalmed. The capstans were also used when man-power alone proved insufficient. 28-22C.

Off to the fishing grounds. The boats heading seawards down the lower harbour could be part of the Penzance fishing fleet which visited Whitby each year until its activities were curtailed during the First World War.   B-37B.

The attraction of this photograph, taken on Tate Hill Pier, lies in its humour, the key figure being the small boy with the expressive face.   19-2A.

"Tempus Fugit." An old fisherman consults his time-piece on Tate Hill Pier. 24-24C.

Again, the natural out-door stage-set of Tate Hill Pier provides the location for this photograph. The girl is Hannah Hall; centre, 'Tin Hat' William Batchelor (also 'Batch'), right 'Cud' Colley. The hats have great character and head-dress of some type is worn by all men photographed out-doors by Sutcliffe. 16-49B.

The contrast of age and youth, always a favourite theme amongst artists. 6-51A.

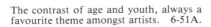

Lizzie Alice Hawksfield holding a 'long line', with a fisherman who has not been identified. She emigrated to Australia when she was thirty and died a few years ago aged 82. Circa 1908. 14-22C.

Three Victorian Misses take an invigorating walk along Pier Road.   26-27C.

Church Street, Whitby, with the Old Town Hall and its clock tower.   3-52B.

Christmas window display of game, poultry and fruit at 87 Church Street, Whitby. Mr Brooksbank would have been the owner around 1910, the probable date of this photograph. Later the business became the property of Matthew Simpson, whose son, Leslie succeeded him and who retired in 1973.   28-39A.

St. Ann's Staith with the drinking fountain presented to the town by Mr R. E. Pannett in 1883.   4-29C.

Stockton Walk, at the junction of Brunswick Street and Flowergate, was demolished circa 1887. The sign above the shop doorway reads 'Sophia Douglas, licensed to deal in game'. 28-27B.

Outside the Board Inn, Church Street. The small boy with bandaged ankle and back to camera is thought to have been William 'Baggy' Austin of the Imperial Inn, Church Street. The double doors in the background are the entrance to Bryant's Rough Jet Warehouse. 28-38C.

Robin Hood's Bay with Ravenscar in the distance. The houses at the extreme left of those on the photograph have since slipped into the sea.   6-58C.

Station Road, Robin Hood's Bay. The Old Police Station, built in the early 1900s replaced the small pan-tiled building at extreme right.   6-59B.

Staithes, with Cowbar Nab in the background.   9-47B.

Staithes, circa 1875. The Cod and Lobster Inn around which figures are grouped in the distance, was washed away in 1882 but since rebuilt.   7-35A.

Runswick from the south-east. 5-8A.

Runswick Bay from the north-west with Kettle Ness in the distance. 5-7B.

East Row, Sandsend. Mr Yeoman with his donkey and cart. Cement works and water driven saw-mill are at the right. 9-17A.

Sandsend, with Low Row cottages and Sandsend Beck. 9-23A.

Staithes and Cowbar Beck from north.   13-25A.

Part of Runswick village.   5-13A.

Chapel Street, Robin Hood's Bay, with Russell's butchers shop on the left. Opposite is Mr Thomas Stubbs standing in the doorway of his bakehouse.   4-7A.

Tin Ghaut, demolished in the 1950s. One of the narrow yards leading direct to the harbour. The ketch 'Mary Jane' is at extreme right. She was a collier owned by Paul Stamp whose coal warehouse was to the right of the boat's bow. She was wrecked at Newholm Beck, two miles from Whitby, on 18th March 1899.   6-70A.

Argument's Yard, Whitby, circa 1895. So named after a Whitby family.   4-43A.

The Old Castle, Mulgrave. This castle probably dates back to shortly after the Norman conquest but there is evidence of a fortified building on the same site dating from Saxon or Roman times. The castle is on the Mulgrave Estate, in the possession of the Marquis of Normanby. 9-41A.

Cottages at Sandsend.   9-7A.

William Batchelor, a sweep who lived in Church Street.   B-32C.

Whitby Abbey. In 658 King Oswy of Northumberland founded a Saxon monastery close to the present site whose first Abbess was St. Hilda. This was destroyed by Vikings but refounded in 1078. What remains of the present Abbey was built over a period extending from the 12th to the 15th centuries.   25-19B.

Beggar's Bridge. The romantic legend built up around this bridge at Glaisdale centres on a poor boy of the village who wished to marry the daughter of a well-to-do family living on the opposite side of the River Esk.

His wooing was discouraged by the girl's father so to prove his merit the boy left home to win the proverbial fortune, did so, returned home and to show that he was now a worthy contender for the girl of his dreams, built this bridge across the Esk.   17-19B.

George Weatherill, (1810-1890), the Whitby artist.   20-33B.

Evelyn and Lulu, two of Frank Sutcliffe's children.   29-21B.

The Power family at Bagdale Old Hall, Whitby.   29-7A.

C. Anderson of Whitby, artist.   27-23B.

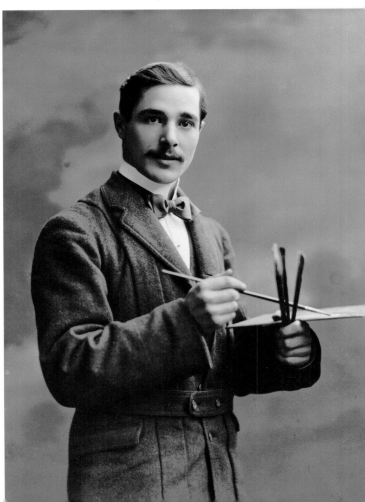

''The Water Rats'' — the most famous of all Frank Sutcliffe's photographs was taken in 1886 and exhibited the following year at the annual exhibition of the Royal Photographic Society of Great Britain. King Edward VII, then Prince of Wales, saw it there and ordered a big enlargement to be made to hang in Marlborough House. That prominence has been given to the fact that the local clergy excommunicated Sutcliffe for showing such an indecent print to the corruption of the other sex has tended at times to divert attention away from the sheer brilliance of this photograph which surely ranks among the top ten photographs of all time. 10-38A.

"Sea Urchins" on the beach near Whitby East Cliff.   24-19D.

"In Puris Naturalibus", taken at Staithes. These photographs, whilst showing mastery of composition and posing, lack much of the spontaneity present in "The Water Rats".   18-49B.

Whitby Friendship Rowing Club. Crew of the four-oared racing gig 'Wild Drake' in 1901 which was launched on 24th June of that year by Miss D. Braithwaite. It was in this boat that the 'Friendship' had many successes over the years.

l. to r.: J. Pearson, T. Henderson, A Thompson (stroke), J. Howard and (seated) R. Coulson (cox).

(Information: courtesy 'Friendship 1879-1951' by W. and W. J. Walker).   30-12B.

A railway cutting under construction at the south-east entrance to Grinkle Tunnel on the Whitby to Stockton via Hinderwell line. Circa 1875.   20-27A.

Sinking the caissons for the Esk Viaduct to carry the Whitby-Scarborough railway line. Circa 1882. 27-12B.

A study of individuals! The staff of Whitby Town Station in 1888.   27-10A.

Opening of the new Swing Bridge at Whitby by Mrs Gervais Beckett on 24th July 1908.   28-16A

Whitby Fire Brigade and appliance at Ruswarp Flour Mill, 24th September 1911. At that time the mill belonged to H. B. Bell Esq. In 1924 it was bought by Thomas H. Hay Esq.   26-41B.

Waterfall on Thorny Beck near Hayburn Wyke, between Robin Hood's Bay and Scarborough.   2-92B.

A country lane with windswept trees. Location unknown.   14-32B.

Ramsdale Mill near Robin Hood's Bay.   8-39A.

At the end of 'The Wizard's Glen' in Mulgrave Woods. The woods, which are in the grounds of Mulgrave Castle, are open to the public at various times during the year.   16-8A.

Thought to be 'The Wishing Stone' in Arncliffe Woods near Glaisdale. So much timber felling and re-growth has taken place since the photograph was taken that it is virtually impossible to make a positive identification.   C-21A.

"Turning Round." Taken in Foulbriggs Field, Lealholm Hall Farm, it shows a North Cave plough being used to row-up potatoes. 10-26B.

A drag harrow being used with a three-horse balk.   14-49B.

Unidentified.   6-73A.

Girl taking turves from a turf stack. Turf was used as a household fuel.   14-38B.

Unidentified.   20-38B.

William Pearson Hodgson with a servant.   20-3A.

Man with a North Cave plough working up to a headland. The plough was manufactured locally of wood with a short iron mould board. The horses are probably a Clydesdale/Shire with possibly some Cleveland Bay in them. Many of the working horses used locally were of a similar variety.   12-44A.

Harvesting barley in a field on Lealholm Hall Farm. George Readman is on the reaper; Bill Readman is stooking; Willie Wren lighting his pipe and Alice Chambers is tying sheaves. 11-10A.

"Haytime 1871." Location unknown. 14-28B.

Lealholm Side with Ben Well House Farm in the background. Nick-named 'Hell-Fire Corner' because of its bleakness. The man with the 'lye' or scythe is probably George Readman of Lealholm Hall Farm. On the blade end of the scythe shaft is the hazel 'bow' which swept the mown corn round in such a way that it was easily gathered into a sheaf with the rake which he is holding in his right hand. At the opposite end of the scythe handle is a 'strickle' for sharpening the blade. 6-76A.

Opening out a field of wheat preparatory to cutting the corn with a horse-drawn reaper. 14-27A.

The scythe in this photograph has an unusually long blade and the handle is of a more recent design than the ones in the other two photographs on this page. 10-15A.

A milk-maid carrying a stool and pail in a field with some fine specimens of Shorthorn cows. 11-37B.

Foulbriggs Field, Lealholm Hall Farm with the Esk Valley in the background. D-24A.

Group with an Ayrshire cow. At that time the Ayrshire was not a common breed in the Whitby district. 29-24A.

George and Isaac Scarth making besoms at Rock Head Cottage, Glaisdale.   4-16B.

Matthew Marwood of Ewe Cote Hall with his milk donkey 'Jane Trotter'.   14-40B.

Frank Morley and his sons of St. Ives Farm, preparing to wash sheep on Fylingdales Moor near the source of the River Derwent. 11-14B.

Willie Coates and his dog near Quarry Farm, Glaisdale with his daughter Eliza standing on the footpath.   19-37A.

Mrs Lythe of Lealholm.   26-4B.

Steeping straw or 'thack' for thatching stacks at Lealholm Hall Farm.   16-51A.

Hoeing or 'singling' turnips at Lealholm Hall Farm.   16-40A.

Unidentified.   14-8A.

At Lealholm Hall Farm.   D-33A.

Stainton Hall Farm, Danby, at that time farmed by Thomas Wilson. This hay-stack had been cut unusually narrow and would have been at risk in a high wind. The hay spade can be seen pushed down into the ledge of hay near the top of the stack. The circular 'staddlin' of stones which formed the base of the stack can be seen behind the poultry.   16-45A.

The River Esk below Ruswarp village and slightly above where the viaduct now stands. We have worked full circle, with some meanderings, from the first three photographs in the book and it is hoped that some impression has been given, both of the rich variety of Frank Meadow Sutcliffe's work and of the area in which he made his home.   16-22D.

HOMAGE TO F. M. SUTCLIFFE

The Whitby that has long gone by
Still lives within your seeing eye,
And we who come beyond your time
Can in imagination climb
The narrow streets and cobbled ways —
That Whitby of those far-off days.
For you have left, that all may share,
Photographs beyond compare,
Of bearded patriarchs of the sea,
And bare-skinned boys who well may be
Of patriarchal age
If they still walk upon life's stage:

And bonny fisher-lasses too,
With many a rare and perfect view
Of harbour side and Abbey plain:
Of misty coast and country lane,
Of great shire horses on the land,
And country men who sturdy stand
To look at us across the years
With such calm eyes, so free from fears,
That now are almost quite unknown
So much the world has lost its own.
Yet, so long as beauty shall survive,
So long will Sutcliffe be alive.

Tom Stamp.

Lily Jackson, the small girl on photograph B-5C (page 27), later became Mrs Stamp, the mother of Tom Stamp whose poem is reproduced above.